Dave Fl

Afterbirth

Methuen Drama

Published by Methuen 2005

1 3 5 7 9 10 8 6 4 2

First published in 2005 by
Methuen Publishing Limited
11–12 Buckingham Gate
London SW1E 6LB

Methuen Publishing Limited Reg. No. 3543167

A CIP catalogue record for this book is available from
the British Library

ISBN 0 413 77562 3

Typeset by Country Setting, Kingsdown, Kent
Printed and bound in Great Britain by
Bookmarque Ltd, Croydon, Surrey

PAIGEWORKS
in collaboration with Arcola Theatre presents

Afterbirth

By Dave Florez
Directed by Deborah Paige

Karim	Kal Aise
Brian	Edward Bennett-Coles
Morris	Robin Berry
Policeman	Chris Chiltern
Muzzy	Craig Blake
Baz	David Judge
Ste	Jumayn Hunter
Madonna	Leila Joyce
Ken	Paul Moriarty
Val	Clara Salaman
Pete	Zak Tallis

Other parts played by members of the company

Director	Deborah Paige
Designer	Atlanta Duffy
Producer	Claudia Woolgar
Lighting Designer	Neil Fraser
Sound Designer	Leon Chambers
Fight Director	Terry King
Assistant Director	Catherine Totty
Assistant Designers	Rhiannon Newman Brown and Alice Walkling
Assistant Lighting Designer	Jack Williams
Deputy Stage Manager	Sara Mcleod
Marketing	Jo Power
Press	Emma Pettit

First produced at Arcola Theatre, September 2005
This text is that used at the start of rehearsals

The Cast

Kal Aise – Karim

Kal trained at the Central School of Speech and Drama, studying an MA in Advanced Theatre Practice, which culminated in a lead performance in *Witness: The Brian Jones Story* at the Embassy Theatre. Student theatre roles at Oxford included Othello, Don John in *Much Ado About Nothing*. Theatre includes: *The Lounge Act*. Film: *New Town Original, Code 46*. TV: *Murder in Mind* and *Canterbury Tales*. As well as corporate and commercial work, together with music videos for innovative new bands like Fourtet and Graffiti, Kal has been involved in many projects with up-and-coming filmmakers, including recently the comic shorts *Blackout* and *A Ticket Too Far*. Kal currently has his own self-penned comedy feature film project *The Baitlands*, in the early stages of development.

Edward Bennett-Coles – Brian

Edward trained at the American Academy of Dramatic Arts in New York where he performed in *Who's afraid of Virginia Woolf, Shadow Box, Bury the Dead, After the Fall, The Marriage of Bette and Boo* and *The Hot I Baltimore*. London theatre includes appearing in Stephen Daldry's production of *Far Away* (Caryl Churchill) at the Royal Court Theatre and the Albery Theatre. Television and film work includes *Rabbit Fever*, a feature due out in the Autumn, *Outside Looking In, Limbo* and *Murder Rooms* for the BBC. Edward is also a member of the Royal Court Writers Programme.

Robin Berry – Morris

Robin graduated from East 15 in 2004. He immediately embarked on a nine month tour of Europe with the highly acclaimed English Theatre Company. He began his professional career before drama school with starring roles in the production of *The Drowned Princess* (Theatre Royal Stratford East) and on television in *Storm Damage* (BBC) directed by Simon Cellan Jones.

Chris Chiltern – Policeman

Chris trained LAMDA. Theatre credits include: *The Comedy of Errors* (Crucible Theatre, Sheffield), *Can't Pay? Won't Pay!* (Derby Playhouse), *The Tempest* (Theatre Royal Bury St Edmunds & UK Tour), *The Mousetrap* (West End), *Lords of the Ring* (Gilded Balloon Edinburgh & Soho Theatre London), *A Midsummer Nights Dream* (Oxford Stage Company), *Tartuffe* (Mobil Touring Theatre), *What The Butler Saw, Absent Friends, Jack and the Beanstalk, Romeo and Juliet, Pygmalion* (Harrogate Theatre). TV: *Family Affairs* (Channel 5), *Casualty, The Queens Nose* (BBC), *Peak Practise, The Waiting Time* (ITV). Film: *The Honeytrap* (Filmhouse).

Craig Blake – Muzzy

Since leaving Rose Bruford Drama School, Craig's film credits include: *Below* (Miramax), *How Stella Got Her Groove Back* (Warner Brothers), *Smile it may Never Happen* (Meltemi Productions). Theatre: *It's Just a Name* (Collective Artistes/ Birmingham Rep), *Four Ladders, Seven Brothers and a Couple of Brooms* (Rough Cut Theatre), *No Sweat* (Birmingham Rep), *Scrape off the Black* (Stratford East Theatre Royal), *Home and Away* (Cardboard Citizens), *Makinde* (Tiata Fahodzi). TV: *Keen Eddie* (Paramount Pictures), *Turkish Delight* (BBC), *The Knock IV* (Bronson and Knight Productions), *Mexican Stand Off* (Johnson Family Films). Craig also works as a freelance drama facilitator for companies including Oval House Theatre, Cardboard Citizens Theatre Company and Lambeth and Southwark Council, recently working on a forum theatre piece for *The Big Life* (Theatre Royal Stratford East).

David Judge – Baz

David trained at East 15 Acting school and with the National Youth Theatre(NYT). His theatre credits include *Citizenship* (National Theatre/The Lowry), *A taste of Honey* (Royal Northern College of Music) and *Kes* (Lyric, Hammersmith).

Jumayn Hunter – Ste

Jumayn is a pupil at Parkview Academy, a specialist school for performing arts and modern languages. Theatre includes: *London Talent '03* (Big Foot LAMDA and RADA), *Macbeth* (Out of Joint) and *Stomp*. He is a drama mentor at his school, loves martial arts and won first place in 'London Enterprise Challenge' for young entrepreneurs.

Leila Joyce – Madonna

Leila trained at The Anna Scher Theatre. Theatre includes: *Honk* (Royal National Theatre), *Peace One Day* (Brixton Academy). Film: *London Birds Can't Fly* (Spirit Dance UK), *Kidscape – Anti Bulling* (Ragdoll Productions). TV: *Canterbury Tales, Are You Looking at Me?, Holby Ciy, Science in Action, Hope & Glory, Trading Places* (BBC), *More Than Love* (Tiger Aspect), *Oops* (Scottish TV), *Anything's Possible* (Channel 5), *Daylight Robbery* (ITV), *The Bill* (ITV1), *Channel 4 Ident Advert* (Channel 4). Radio: *The Bed and Breakfast Star* (BBC Radio 4).

Paul Moriarty – Ken

Theatre includes: *King Lear* directed by Trevor Nunn, *Penny For A Song, Anthony and Cleopatra, Troilus and Cressida, Bingo, Dingo, Destiny, Captain Swing, Twelfth Night, The Tempest* (all RSC), *Sing Your Heart out for the Lads, The David Hare Trilogy, As I Lay Dying, The Murderers, Macbeth, Black Snow, The Crucible*, working with William Gaskill, Richard Eyre and Peter Gill (all RNT), *Kingfisher Blue* (The Bush), *A Patch of Blue* (Kings Head), *Peter Pan* (Rickmansworth), *Appetite* (Theatre Royal Windsor), *All My Sons* (Colchester), *The Contractor* (Oxford Stage Co), *A View From The Bridge* directed by Deborah Paige, *Oi for England* (Royal Court), *Elizabeth I* (Royal Court), *Serious Money* (Wyndhams, New York) and *Mysteries (God)* Lyceum).
TV: *Holby City, Jack of Hearts, Pride and Prejudice, Eastenders (Regular – George), Paradise Club Murder Most Horrid* (BBC), *Touch of Frost, Comic Strip, Troilus and Cressida, South of the Border, Saracens, Maigret, The Bill,*

The Gentle Touch (LWT), *The Knock* (Thames). Paul has also had leading roles in *Wycliffe, Minder, The Sweeney, Between the Lines* and *Peak Practice*.

Clara Salaman – Val

Clara trained at Central School of Speech and Drama. Theatre includes: *Popcorn* (National Tour), *Mill on the Floss* (Shared Experience), *King Lear* (Crucible Theatre, Sheffield), *Prin* (West Yorkshire Playhouse), *Sweet Charity* and *Don Juan* (Harrogate Theatre), *The Great Pretenders* (Gate), also the title roles in *Courting Winona* (Old Red Lion), *Emma* (King's Head) and *Lulu* (Red Shift Theatre Company). TV: *The Bill* (Thames) for which she was nominated for Best Newcomer in the National TV Awards, *Beech is Back* (Thames), *William and Mary, Holby City, Old Devils, A Fatal Inversion* (all BBC), *Bad Girls* (Shed), *The Playground* (CBBC), *Heartbeat* (YTV), and *Maigret* (Granada).

Zak Tallis – Pete

Zak is a pupil at Parkview Academy in North London, a specialist school for performing arts and modern languages. He has previously worked with *Chicken Shed Theatre*; *Afterbirth* is his first professional production.

The Crew

Monique Briggs – Chaperone / Production Assistant

Monique was granted a Bachelor of Education, majoring in Drama in 1994. In 1996 she initiated her own theatre company – Zip Antics – and has managed, produced and acted with this company for the past nine years. Since living in London she has produced for Zip Antics (Brighton Fringe, Nuffield Theatre and Jermyn Street Theatre), The Hobbs Factory and MOOT Theatre Company at the Edinburgh Fringe. She has also started her own production company under the name MONSTAR Productions.

Leon Chambers – Sound Designer

Leon has spent 18 years working with sound. He has recorded and edited over 200 hours of radio drama for BBC Radio 4, and Radio 3 including for Simon Callow, Sir Peter Hall and Max Stafford-Clark. *Laughter in the Dark* (Catherine Bailey Productions) won Gold in the 2005 Sony Radio Drama Awards. *The Permanent Way* (Catherine Bailey Productions) won Silver. In addition to radio drama he produces audio recordings for Oxford University Press and has made three short films in the last two years; *Dial 'M' for Mother*, *The Bank Job*, and *The Match*.

Atlanta Duffy – Designer

Atlanta trained at Motley Theatre Design School and the Lyric Theatre, Hammersmith. She has designed for: Bristol Old Vic, Lyric Theatre, Hammersmith, West Yorkshire Playhouse, Wilton's Music Hall, Tricycle Theatre, Southwark Playhouse, BAC, The King's Head, Stephen Joseph Theatre, Bath Theatre Royal, Birmingham Rep, Oxford Playhouse and the Muson Theatre, Lagos. Previous work with Deborah Paige includes *Trojan Women* and *A Month in the Country* (RADA), *Electra* (Arts Ed) and *Don Giovanni* (ETO). For the Arcola she has designed *Come Out Eli* –Time Out Fringe First Award, *Inside Out* Dir. Natasha Betteridge, Clean Break Theatre Co, and *Sense of Belonging* Dir. Chuck Mike. She is currently designing *The Lion and the Jewel* for the Barbican's Young Genius Season.

Dave Florez – Writer

Dave has been part of the Young Writer's Programmes at the Royal Court, Soho Theatre and Paines Plough. This is his first full-length play.

Neil Fraser – Lighting Designer

Neil is RADA's director of Technical Training. He studied Drama at Manchester University. As Resident Designer at Contact, work inculdes: *When the Wind Blows*, *The Doctor and the Devils*, *The Breadshop The Wedding* and *Mowgli's Jungle*. He became Head of Lighting at RADA in 1985 and has lit many productions for the Academy around the UK and abroad. He has worked with Sheffield Crucible, Polka Children's Theatre, Library Theatre Manchester, Donmar Warehouse, Paines Plough and the Westminster Theatre. Off-Broadway: *Bloody Poetry* for director Chris Hayes, and more than ten pieces for William Gaskill. Neil has worked with: Nona Shepherd, Andrew Visnevski, Geoff Bullen, Deborah Paige, and Robin Midgley. He recently lit *Blithe Spirit* and *Macbeth* at Derby Playhouse, for Karen Hebden. Neil is author of: *Sound and Lighting for the Theatre* (1988), *Stage Lighting Design: A Practical Guide* (1999), *Stage Lighting Explained* (2002) and *Theatre History Explained* (2004). *The Complete Handbook of Theatre Lighting* is due out in late 2005, and is co-written by colleague and former pupil Simon Bennison of the Royal Opera, Covent Garden. This is to be followed by a beginner's guide to the *Life, Times and Works of William Shakespeare* (due early 2006).

Sara McLeod – Deputy Stage Manager

Sara has recently worked as Deputy Stage Manger to William Gaskill on *Carver* (Arcola) and on *The Beach* (Theatre 503). She was Stage Manager on *Jaques and his Master* (White Bear), *Shortcuts '05* (Arcola) and *Breshnev's Children* (Diorama). Sara studied at Queen Margaret University College and London Metropolitan University where she was Assistant Stage Manager on *The Break of Day* and *Travellator*.

Rhiannon Newman Brown – Assistant Designer

Rhiannon has just graduated from Motley Theatre Design Course. Prior to this she graduated from the University of Leeds with BA Hons in History of Art in 2002. She has worked as ASM/DSM at Glynebourne Opera House for 2 years and with Howard Eaton Lighting Ltd making pieces for West End Productions.

Deborah Paige – Director

Deborah started her directing career at the Bristol Old Vic, Soho Theatre Company and Salisbury Playhouse, where she was Artistic Director from 1990 to 1994. There, her production of *For Services Rendered* transferred to The Old Vic in London, *Twelfth Night* was invited to The Shanghai Shakespeare Festival, and Sam Shepard's *States of Shock* (British Premiere) was part of the Royal National Theatre's Springboard season (1993). Other productions include: *A Midsummer Night's Dream*, *The Tempest*, *Private Lives*, *A Winter's Tale*, *Wild Things*, *Relative Values* and *The Entertainer*. In 1995 she was appointed Artistic Director of The Crucible, Sheffield, where productions included *King Lear*, *The Merchant of Venice*, *Mojo*, *Hay Fever*, *South Pacific*, *Blue Remembered Hills*, *Way Upstream* and *A View From The Bridge*. She premiered *Villette* and *Queuing for Everest*, two new works by Judith Adams and *Brassed Off* (world stage premiere) transferred to the Royal National Theatre in 1993. She has also worked at Hampstead Theatre, The Open Air theatre in Regents Park, the Wolsey Theatre, Ipswich, Theatre Centre, London, the ICA and the Edinburgh Festival. She now works as a free-lance director in theatre, opera and television and radio: (including *Don Giovanni (*ETO); *EastEnders*, *Casualty* and *Judge John Deed (*BBC), *Only In London and Speed* and *Silver* for *(*BBC Radio 4*)*. Deborah regularly directs at RADA and LAMDA. Pursuing her commitment to new and original work for theatre, she formed her own company, PAIGEWORKS in 2005. *Afterbirth* is its first production.

Catherine Totty – Assistant Director

Catherine's professional work as director includes *The Zoo Story* and *Krapp's Last Tape* (John Gielgud Theatre). She has been assistant director to Howard Barker on *The Fence in its Thousandth Year* (Birmingham Rep and Tour), Mark Wing-Davey on *Passions* (Tristan Bates), William Gaskill on *Bloomsday Readings*, Nick Hutchison on *The Knight of the Burning Pestle*, Tony Graham on *Coram Boy Reading* and Gari Jones on *Biloxi Blues* (Vanburgh Theatre). She recently production managed *Carver* (Arcola). Prior to training at RADA on the Theatre Technical Arts Course, Catherine studied a Master of Physics degree at Oxford University, directing many productions including *Little Shop of Horrors* (Oxford Playhouse). She was a short-listed director for Old Vic *24 Hour Plays*.

Alice Walkling – Assistant Designer

Alice has just graduated from Motley Theatre Design Course, before which she studied English Literature at the University of East Anglia. She spent a year assisting the Design Team at Maddermarket Theatre in Norwich on productions including *A Doll's House* and *Henry V*. She also worked on costume for a BBC programme about Thomas Hardy.

Jack Williams – Assistant Lighting Designer

Jack is a graduate of RADA. He is pleased to return to the Arcola where he was assistant lighting designer on *Carver* in July. This is the forth time he has worked with Neil Fraser: previous work includes co-lighting designer on *A Winter's Tale* and *The America Play* (RADA) directed by William Gaskill earlier this year. In 2003 Jack lit the *Crossing Path* at the Cottesloe NT as part of the Shell Connections Youth Theatre. Recent work includes lighting & sound designer on *Animal Farm* at the Broadway Theatre, Barking and the Edinburgh Fringe Festival.

The Arcola Theatre

The Arcola Theatre, was founded by Mehmet Ergen, the present artistic director, in September 2000 when he converted a textile factory on the borders of Stoke Newington /Dalston into one of London's largest and most adaptable fringe venues. In just five years it has become one of the country's most renowned fringe theatres with a distinct and powerful identity both within in its local community and the British theatre.

Since its foundation, Arcola has won the Peter Brook Empty Space Award two years in a row and was given the Time Out Live Award for 2003. A large number of its productions have been selected as Time Out Critic's Choice. It has gained a reputation for staging work by some of the best contemporary writers and directors, including productions by Dominic Droomgoole, Max Stafford-Clark, David Farr, Bill Gaskill, Adam Rapp, Sam Shepard and Eric Schossler.

Arcola does not receive regular core funding from any organisation and at present the vast majority of its staff work on a voluntary basis. Most are theatre professionals who dedicate their valuable time and energy to a project they passionately believe in.

Artistic Director:	Mehmet Ergen
General Manager:	Leyla Nazli
Co-Manager:	Ben Todd
Associate Director:	Serdar Bilis
Associate Producer:	Philip Arditti
Box Office Manager:	David Luff
Press and Marketing:	Mobius Industries
Literary Assosiate:	Alison Weston

www.arcolatheatre.com

Afterbirth

Characters

Ken, *fifty*
Ste, *thirteen*
Pete, *twelve*
Baz, *fourteen*
Val, *thirty-five*
Morris, *twenty-one*
Pupil, *fourteen*
Policeman, *forty*
Madonna, *thirteen*
Muzzy, *thirty*
Karim, *twenty-eight*
Brian, *thirty-five*
Keith, *twenty-one*
Gerbil, *thirty*
Katie, *thirty*
Steven, *thirty-six*
Policewoman, *twenty-seven*

Scene One

October. Burnt Oak, north-west London.

It is midnight. Round the back of the MFI car park, by the train tracks. A patch of green, a dustbin and a bench. Beneath the orange glow of the streetlights sits **Ken**, *a fifty-year-old man in a lumberjack shirt, brown leather jacket and corduroys. He drinks from a bottle of Wray & Nephew which he passes around.* **Ste** *takes a hit: he's thirteen at most, and is wearing a Kangol jumper with its hood over a Yankees cap and baggy jeans. He holds a plastic bag in one hand.* **Pete** *is twelve, although he could be younger; he wears a black bomber-jacket, Nike woolly hat and baggy jeans. His voice is unbroken and he too holds a plastic bag. The boys walk around, gob on the ground and occasionally jump on the bench to keep warm.* **Ken** *just sits there.*

Ken How much they going for?

Ste Tenner. Maybe more. I know a bloke can get it for free. Mate does the recording.

Pete That's rank. *Gang Bang Granny.* How long is it?

Ken I'll have one.

Pete How long is it?

Ste That'll be a tenner.

Ken Said you can get it for free.

Ste *I* can. For you it's a tenner.

Pete How much is it? Sorry, how long is it?

Ken Fiver.

Ste Eight.

Ken Three quid.

Ste Fiver, done.

Ken Don't believe ya.

Pete How *fucking* long is it?

Ste Long enough! They ring at the door, she answers, pop, drag her to the living room, Lee takes out her teeth, sticks it in, Rich cuts off her clothes, strips her. They got lube, up her arse, in her fanny. No, no, hang on a minute, there's about ten minutes, that's right, he gets, he buggers her with a bottle of Beck's and then puts a condom on a cucumber for some reason and stuffs that up her . . .

Pete Bollocks!

Ken *offers smokes. They take and he lights them.*

Ste Swear *down* blood! Got a whole bag of stuff *and* they're masked up. Then they sperm on her, trash the place, nick the tele and shit and leave her for dead. Least I *think* she died. Dunno if she died. Musta snuffed it.

Ken And all this cos she grassed up next door.

Ste Next door the other one, next door that, the Calderwoods. I *told* you they're fucking mashed.

Ken What old lady deserves that?

Pete *sits on* **Ken**'s *lap to hear the story.*

Ste Dunno the ins and outs, but she rang the feds about them stashing goods at Number 12, so they mugged her pension outside the PO before she could get in the taxi. I think that's how Luke got inside, she ID'd him at the station, he got done for grievous, so his brothers taught her a lesson. What else happened fuck knows, all I know is copies are going for tenners all over the estate, maybe more.

Ken I'll reserve judgement till I see it.

Ste Believe, Ken, I thought I was gonna see an episode of *Neighbours*, know what I mean? Stuck it in, nearly ralphed. They use a tripod and everything . . . not under the camera, on *her*. There's this white cream that oozes out her arse, must've had piles, fuck knows, it's not for wanking, but could be a market, Rich is making a killing.

Silence. They smoke.

Ken (*checks watch*)   Should be here by now.

Ste   Probably got trapped at home.

Pete *inhales from the plastic bag.*

Ken   What time you gotta go?

Ste   Doesn't get busy till half-past.

Ken   And you?

Pete   I'll go with Ste.

Ste *inhales from bag.*

Ken   Give you guys a lift.

Pete   We'll walk, 'salright.

Ken   Don't tell me, I cramp your style.

Pete   Well, you are a bit of a cunt.

Ken *gets* **Pete** *in a headlock and takes off his woolly hat.*

Ste   Dutch haircut!

Ken   Would the jury spokesman please stand up?

Ste *stands to attention.*

Ken .   Has the jury reached a verdict?

Ste   Yes, your honour.

Ken   Is the verdict unanimous?

Ste   Yes, your honour.

Ken   And what is the verdict?

Ste   Guilty.

Ken   Pardon?

Ste   Guilty!

Ken   Oh right, in that case, I hereby sentence you to a dutch haircut.

Ste Ten dutch haircuts!

Ken Ten dutch haircuts. Are you ready?

Pete *is still struggling.* **Ken** *quickly rubs his knuckles on the top of* **Pete**'s *head.*

Ken One, two, three, four, five, six, seven, eight, nine, ten.

Pete Aaargh!

Pete *runs up to* **Ste** *and kicks him.* **Ste** *kicks him back.* **Pete** *threatens to kick* **Ken**.

Ken Now boys, stop it!

Baz *enters. He wears a Kappa top and baggy jeans. He is fourteen max. He sets down his small duffle bag and surveys the skirmish.*

Ste Hey! Baz, man! Come here, ya fucking prick!

Ste *hugs* **Baz**.

Pete Right Baz? I just had ten dutch haircuts.

Ken Next time it's a Chelsea smile. Ya finally made it.

Baz Ken. (*To* **Ste**.) Gi's a hit.

Ste Ask Pete.

Baz Pete.

Pete 'King hell, man.

Baz *takes a hit from* **Pete**'s *bag.*

Ste So? How was it? You went to a different one. Way out in sticks. Me and Anish tracked ya down. Looked like a fucking castle.

Baz Don't wanna talk about it now. Passed the park. Ya weren't there.

Ste Just came for a breather. 'King packed down there.

Pete No it weren't.

Ste Yes it were.

Ken   Sit down. Take the weight off your Filas.

Ken *offers a smoke.* **Baz** *takes one and sits down.*

Ste   'King missed shit-loads mate. Cops took Malcolm away. Grassed up by his own bird. Means we gotta buy from Danish Dave, he's only got resin, not even the good stuff, proper dog shit. He should be out soon, Mal, but fuck knows, he's got previous. Dave's all the way over on Albatross, 'king trek I tell ya. Ya must've found some contacts, no one from Grahame Park in the castle?

Slight pause.

Baz   Does he ever shut up?

Ken *laughs.* **Ste** *gives the finger.*

Ste   Right, Pete. See ya guys down the park. You *are* coming?

Baz   Got fuck-all else.

Ste   If it's anything like last night, we'll be rolling in it. Good to have ya back, Baz.

Baz   Good to be back.

Pete *gives* **Ken** *a little kick and legs it with* **Ste**.

Ken   That's it, ya little turd. I'm giving ya a full-on smile next time!

He takes out a fag and lights it.

Silence.

I missed ya.

Baz *nods and takes a drag.*

Silence.

Ken *gets up to walk off.*

Baz   Where ya going?

Ken   Gonna give ya lift back.

Baz Where?

Ken Your gaff.

Baz Don't wanna go back yet. Sit down. Take the weight off your Clarks.

He sits. They smoke in silence.

Ken How come they let ya back? They had enough or did Mum ask?

Baz Val said it would be OK. And they had enough. She only wants me back to help out with the baby.

Ken So I heard. Boy or girl?

Baz Alan. Bit of a weak name really. S'pose I had to come back. Curious.

Slight pause.

Ken What do ya get up to over there?

Baz Look, I *tried* to come back. To get back to work and stuff, but it was over in Highwood Hill and I was getting in enough shit as it was . . .

Ken Sssssh, ssssh, it's alright, I understand.

Baz So they put me with a couple of fosters. First pair were shite. Second lot were better. Uncle Inglis and Auntie Maureen. But they got full so I had to go back. If it's between the home and here, I choose here every time, you know that don'tcha.

Ken Course. Hey, come here . . .

*He puts an arm around **Baz**.*

Ya must be freezing ya balls off in that.

Baz I'm fine.

Baz *takes a swig of the rum.*

Ken I saved something for ya. Call it a welcoming present.

Ken *takes a bag of weed out his pocket.* **Baz** *takes it and quickly puts it in his jeans pocket.* **Baz** *starts to massage* **Ken***'s groin.* **Ken** *eventually breaks off.*

Ken   Need a cash machine. I'll drive us to the park. And then . . . no, *then*, I give ya lift back home to face the music. Ya gotta do it some point.

Baz   S'pose.

A train comes by very near and fast. The place lights up with white flashes. **Baz** *picks up his bag and walks off.* **Ken** *gives it a bit and then follows him.*

Scene Two

A council flat in Grahame Park estate. A TV, couch and armchair in the living room. The kitchen is to one side. On the counter are a toaster and a kettle. Bare white walls, peeling and damp at the corners. There is an electricity meter by the front door. Beyond the front door is an iron grille. A baby's cot sits on a table by the wall. **Val** *sits on the armchair smoking a fag and watching the match. She has the shakes a little. She wears a Champion top and Adidas joggers.* **Baz** *stands holding a can of Coke and a KitKat, watching* **Alan** *in the cot.* **Val** *nervously looks at* **Baz**.

Val   You gonna stand there all day?

Baz *sips.*

Val   It doesn't like being stared at.

Baz   How d'ya know?

Beat.

Val   Stop being creepy and sit yourself down.

Baz   Val . . .

Val   If you ask me one more question about that baby so help me God I'll get my Mark round here. I've just got him off, now do us all a favour and sit the fuck.

Baz *sits on the far end of the couch and watches the match.*

Silence.

She stares at him, drinking the Coke; he stares at the TV.

Val   You finished with that Coke yet?

Baz *shakes his head.*

Val   Like I say, I'll throw it away for ya.

Long pause.

Val   Give us the wrapper, I'll bin it.

Baz   Don't want sticky fingers. Thanks anyway.

Slight pause.

Val   Brian said you weren't in last night. Rang the bell. No answer. Should've been home. Where were ya?

Baz   Out. Where were you?

Val   Maxine's with the baby. Needed *some* help, didn't I?

Baz   Well you've got your baby-sitter now, haven't ya? So relax.

Pause.

Val   You ready for school tomorrow?

Baz *nods.*

Val   You finished with that Coke yet?

Baz *shakes his head.*

Slight pause.

Baz   Can I hold the baby now?

Val   Sleeping.

Baz   When it wakes.

Val   It doesn't wake. It just sleeps. It only wakes when I'm sleeping. Anyway, I know you, you'll drop it on its head.

Baz *drains the Coke and crushes it beyond repair in his hand, while looking at* **Val***'s reaction.* **Val** *does her best not to explode. He offers it to her.*

Baz   Finished.

Slight pause.

There is the sound of a motorcycle pulling up outside. Then a ring at the doorbell. Suddenly dogs start to bark loudly from behind the closet door next to the front door. They are most probably two or three large, vicious Alsatians. **Val** *gets up, still staring daggers at* **Baz***, and checks through the spy-hole.*

Val   Wait a minute!

She opens a small metal box next to the electricity meter and presses a few buttons. The sound of the dogs gradually stops. She undoes numerous bolts and locks, opens the front door and then unlocks the iron grille in front of that. **Morris** *storms in and goes up to the cot. He is twenty-one max, wears a biker's jacket and jeans, and is carrying his helmet. The purr of the motorcycle continues outside.*

Morris   Lost me key . . . fuck! I knew it!

Val   What?

Morris   It's black! Ya spawned a fucking monkey!

Val   It's not black! How is *that* black!

Morris   Are you blind as well as dumb?! What fucking colour is *that* when it's at home?!

Val   Don't shout, you'll wake it up!

Morris   Why did you have to lie?! Think I wouldn't find out?! I'm not colour-blind! It's the ace of cunting spades!

Val   You obviously are blind! Look at it!

Morris *storms out the flat. The sound of the motorcycle is cut dead.*

Val   Baz! Baz, you saw it, it ain't black is it?!

Baz *ignores her.*

Morris *storms back in holding an industrial-strength torch. He shines it into the cot.*

Morris   What the fuck colour is that?

Val   It's not black, it's . . . tanned.

Morris   And where did it get *that* from, I wonder.

Val   Er . . . hello?

Val *steps back to show her pale, pasty white body to* **Morris**.

Beat.

Morris   If I find out it's Muzzy's or Karim's I'm gonna shoot them and then I'm gonna shoot you.

Val   For the last fucking time! It's not theirs! It's Mark's! It's mine!

Morris   Should *bleach* the fucker if you think it's white.

Val   Bleach you if you're not careful, put it in your fucking *pipe*.

Morris   I'm trying to help ya, that's all. It means cash, dunnit, support. I could have a quiet word with Karim, I'm sure he wouldn't . . .

Val   You and your quiet words. How's this for a quiet word: FUCK OFF OUT OF 'ERE.

The baby starts crying. They stare at each other. Eventually, **Morris** *walks calmly towards the door.*

Val   Ain't ya gonna say hello to ya brother?

Morris *turns and notices* **Baz**. **Baz** *continues to watch the TV.* **Morris** *turns to walk out the door.*

The baby still cries. **Baz** *turns up the volume to the TV.*

Val   Ya finished with your KitKat?

Baz *gets up, finishes off the KitKat, crumbles the shiny wrapper into a ball and puts it in his pocket. He walks out of the door.*

Val *stares at the crying baby.*

Lights fade.

The crying gets louder.

Filling the auditiorium.

Scene Three

Baz *is at school. He sits at a desk writing an essay. Another* **Pupil** *sits at the desk next to him, also writing.*

Pupil *jogs* **Baz**. **Baz** *looks at him, smiles a little and gets back to work.*

Beat.

Pupil *jogs him again.* **Baz** *doesn't look up. Mildly frustrated.*

As soon as he goes to write again . . . jog. His pen makes a huge mark on the paper. Ruining all he's written.

Pause. **Baz** *looks at* **Pupil**, *who pretends to get on with his work.*

Baz *writes some more.* **Pupil** *gives it a bit and then jogs again.*

Baz *smiles hopelessly at the situation. He goes to write again – jog.*

And again – jog.

And again – jog.

He looks at **Pupil**, *who looks back confrontationally at* **Baz**.

Baz *backs down and continues writing. A futile gesture.*

Jog.

Blackout.

Scene Four

The flat. **Madonna** *is thirteen. She wears a silver puffa jacket and ripped jeans. She leans up against the wall, chewing bubble gum. A* **Policeman** *in full uniform sits on the couch having a cup of tea.*

Policeman   This tea's shit.

Beat.

It's like mud. Mud and piss. Did you piss in this?

Pause.

It's freezing in here. She should save some of the crack money for tokens. Baby will die otherwise. I've seen it. Pneumonia. Hypothermia. Poor fucker. Doesn't stand a chance, that one. Can't wait to put him inside. From the crib to the nick. I give it twelve years. Looks black and all. Know who the father is?

Silence.

When you find out let me know. I could do with a laugh. Sit down, you're making me nervous.

She doesn't. She blows a bubble.

How are the brothers? How's Morris? Been quiet lately. Getting ready for a big one?

Pause.

Don't worry, wouldn't expect you to grass your own family. Leave that to your mother. How is Val?

Pause.

Madonna. Why you dicking me about?

You see, the way I see it is, I'm doing my side and you're . . . *dicking* me about. If you keep telling me little porkies, the Chief Constable's gonna catch on. Not that he really cares in the first place, but it looks bad on me, I'll never make plain clothes at this rate, but that's not the point. Point is, I may just get tired of you and your *information*. May just start treating you like every other cunt on the estate. It's a domino-effect see. You start wasting my time with unnecessary paper work and I start blacking up your hands and your punters. It's tit for tat. We've been there, done that, let's not do it again, please. Let's keep the status, alright?

She blows another bubble.

Got a kilo of brown in the other week. Big shipment at the Marshes. Probably heard about that. We got there first. No thanks to you. Be a shame to see all that gather dust now, wouldn't it?

He throws a bag of crack on the floor.

She hurries to get it.

Er . . .

She stops in her tracks.

She kneels on the floor, puts her hands behind her back and picks it up with her teeth. She stands up and drops the package into her hand and puts it in her pocket. This process is carried out teasingly slowly. He looks at her all the while. His concentration is suddenly broken by sounds coming from next door. The neighbours have kicked off again.

Christ, do they ever pack it in?

He pats the seat next to him

She sits.

He sticks his hand into her jacket and gropes her breasts.

Piss in my tea.

Pause.

I know it costs extra. That *is* extra. Piss in my tea.

She blows a bubble. He pops it with a finger.

We'll play games another time. All I want is exactly the same as your regulars. Can't be too much to ask, can it? Little bird's told me everything. You should've seen my face. Like a Cheshire Cat I was.

He affectionately taps her nose.

Anyway, didn't mean to surprise you like this. Was only passing. Ain't seen you around in months. What it is? Four, five? Thought you'd done a runner. Was beginning to miss

ya. I'm a soppy thing. Good to have you back, though.
Gonna walk me to the door?

They get up. She opens the door for him. He puts on his helmet.

He holds his hand out for her to spit out the gum. She does.

He spits on her face. Then he wipes it off with a handkerchief.

Just remember what you are.

He exits.

As she is about to close the iron grille **Baz** *walks in in school uniform.*

Baz   What's *he* doing here?

Madonna *wipes her face.*

Madonna   Wanted to know where Morris was.

Baz   Where's Val?

Madonna   Fuck knows.

Baz *checks up on* **Alan**.

Baz   He's got dribble all over his chin.

He wipes it with the cuff of his jumper.

You shouldn't put so many toys by his head. Ain't you 'eard
of cot death?

Madonna   Don't be giving me ideas.

Baz *takes* **Alan** *out of the cot and sits next to* **Madonna** *on the
couch.*

Madonna   You shouldn't be picking him up.

Baz   Hey, watch this . . .

He makes some clicking noises with his mouth.

Aah, he usually does it. Here. Hold him.

Madonna   He stinks. Get him away from me.

Baz   You were once a little baby.

Madonna   I don't remember that.

Baz   He's got your eyes.

Madonna   'K off.

Baz   He *has*, look.

Tentatively she opens the cloth around his head a bit.

Madonna   Same colour, maybe.

Baz   And the rest.

Madonna *gives a closer look.*

Baz   Hold him.

She nearly succumbs, but suddenly gets up and takes her keys from the table.

Madonna   Should put him back. You'll get in trouble.

Baz   Stay a bit.

Madonna   I'm out o' here. Your turn to be nanny.

Madonna *leaves.*

Baz *gets up.*

Baz   Wait. Madge. Madge!

He puts the baby back in the cot and puts the chain on the door.

*He picks **Alan** up again, carefully.*

Hello, Buster, eh? Hello. (**Baz** *sniffs a bit under the baby and pulls a face.*) Just you and me now. Ssssh, sssh. What's my name, eh? Huh? *Yeah*, that's right, Baz. Short for Barry. And your name's Al. Short for Alan. And when ya older you'll be called Big Al. That's a fuck-off name, innit? Big Al. Say that again. (**Baz** *puts his ear close to **Alan**.*) Ya can't concentrate with all that racket? Don't blame ya, mate.

He takes him over to the far wall to listen to the bickering couple next door.

We know what they're called, don't we? Go on, go on. (*He puts his ear close again.*) Exactly. Steve Marmoor and Katie Fisher. Steve's just been let out of . . . Pentonville, that's right. Manslaughter – it was really murder, but he made it look like an accident. She's talking about it now. He really hates it when that happens, listen. He's gonna start throwing things soon – there. Told ya. Smashing plates, ashtrays, all sorts of stuff. Now it's her turn to go ballistic. She usually jumps on him. And tries to choke him. He knocks her down and that's when the punching starts . . . Any minute now . . .

They listen. On cue, we hear him punch her repeatedly. The knocks and the shrieks.

That there is the sound of true love.

There are sounds at the door. **Baz** *quickly puts the baby back in the cot and turns on the TV.* **Val** *opens the door but the chain is on.* **Baz** *unhooks the chain.*

Val *enters with* **Muzzy** *and* **Karim**. *They are carrying her shopping. They both wear parkas with the hoods up.*

Val   Why's the chain on?

Baz   Be on the safe side.

Val *puts some tokens in the electricity meter.*

Val (*to* **Muzzy** *and* **Karim**)   What ya waiting for? Ya know where they go.

Muzzy *and* **Karim** *walk over to the kitchen.*

Muzzy (*as in 'hello'*)   Baz.

Baz   What.

Beat.

Muzzy   Hello.

Baz *just stares at him.*

Karim (*to* **Muzzy**)   Come on, move.

They take their hoods down and unload the shopping in the fridge and cupboards.

Val   Why ain't the dogs barking?

Baz   Dunno. Madonna musta turned it off.

Val   Where is she? Supposed to be looking after the kid.

Baz   Gone out.

Val   Where?

Baz *shrugs, still eyeing the other two. He lights a fag.*

Val *looks into the cot.*

Val   She didn't clean him up. Give him a new nappy. It shit itself.

Baz   I don't know how to . . .

Val *walks into the bathroom.*

Val (*offstage*)   I'm having a bath.

Beat.

Karim (*to* **Baz**)   Don't mind us.

Muzzy *laughs.*

Baz *walks to the front door, opens it and leans against the door frame.*

Baz   Whenever ya ready, guys.

Muzzy *and* **Karim** *clock* **Baz** *and take their time putting the shopping back.*

Muzzy   Bit nippy in 'ere, innit?

Karim   Must be a draught somewhere.

Muzzy   Telling *me*. Got it down ma *neck* man. Where's it coming from?

Karim   Beats me, Muzz.

Muzzy, *in over-the-top style, suddenly sees the gaping door.*

Muzzy   Baz, man! The door! Getting *bear* draughts in 'ere blood!

Karim *starts laughing.*

Baz *inhales a deep drag.*

Muzzy (*theatrically*)   Brrr, shivers down the *bones*! Come Kaz, finish up, gonna freeze ma dick off in 'ere.

Muzzy *goes up to the bathroom door.*

Muzzy   Laters yeah, all done. Scrub up and get buff, alright!

Val (*offstage*)   Yeah, yeah!

Karim   All done, ya royal highness! Hostess with the mostess!

Muzzy *and* **Karim** *slowly walk over to the door, pretending to be afraid of* **Baz.** *They keep as much distance as possible away from him as they exit.* **Karim** *makes a sharp exit.* **Muzzy** *takes out a little cuddly toy with the price tag still on from his parka. He offers it to* **Baz** *as a peace offering.*

Muzzy   For da bubba.

Baz *takes the toy.* **Muzzy** *exits.* **Baz** *closes the door, walks up to the bin and throws the toy into it.*

Baz *takes a deep breath and goes up to the cot, fag in mouth. He manages to undo the nappy on the baby and slowly take it out, desperately trying to keep all the contents in. He folds it up and holds it at arm's length. He goes to the bin, but it is full. He opens the window and flings it out. He wipes his hands on his top.*

Baz   I don't *know* how to put a nappy on!

Val (*offstage*)   Figure it out!

Baz *takes a nappy from the packet on the floor. He reads the instructions and puts his fag down in the ashtray on the couch. He waves some of the smoke away with his hand. He gets some wipes out and cleans the baby. Grimacing and holding his breath all the while. He drops the used wipes to the floor and shakes talcum powder on the*

baby, *probably more than he should. He puts on the new nappy as
quickly as possible. Figuring he could probably just get away with what
he's created, he tucks in the baby and gives him a kiss. He throws the
wipes out of the window and shuts it. He leans on the table and bows
his head to get his breath back. He picks up the fag, puts his jacket on
and knocks on the bathroom door.*

Val *opens the bathroom door ajar. She is obviously naked offstage.*

Baz *averts his eyes.*

Baz   Mum!

Val (*offstage*)   What?!

Baz (*looking away*)   I'm going out for a bit so keep an eye on
Al.

Val (*offstage*)   Take your time, I'm having mates over.

He looks across at the baby and gives a quick wave.

He exits.

Scene Five

Baz, **Ste** *and* **Pete** *are standing on the corner of Hundred Acre,
outside the public toilets. It is around nine p.m. They are virtually in
darkness. Now and then headlights of cars light them up as they pass
by. They are sharing a huge bag of pic'n'mix sweets; full of jelly snakes
and spiders, strawberry lips, dracula teeth, fried eggs and Coke bottles.*
Baz *writes his tag on the 'Gents' sign with a thick black marker: it
reads 'GranZey'.*

Baz   Alan's gonna be a DJ. He told me last night.

Ste   If he can talk already he should be an MC.

Pete *laughs and bites the head off a jelly snake after dangling it over
his mouth.*

Baz   Nah, MC you gotta be lucky, gotta be born with it.
DJ he can learn the ropes. Get the decks, get a system . . .

A car goes by. In the headlights **Baz** *flashes his genitals.* **Pete** *makes a slow wanking gesture with his hand. They wait for the car to stop. It doesn't.*

Ste   Cos *that's* easy, getting a system.

Baz   It's all about contacts. Not what you know, *who* you know. And who knows you. That's the trick. It's all about power. Respect. Get the women. Get the gold.

Ste   Hark at the breh!

Baz   Too right. Alan's gonna be the fucking Gate-Master. Spin it at the Dungeon. Spin it at Venom. Have to ask his *permission* to get into Pussy Cat.

Another car passes. In the headlights **Ste** *jumps on* **Baz**'s *back and* **Pete** *moons. They look and wait. Nothing.*

Baz   Get off!

Ste   I'm bored anyway. Run out o' glue. So has Pete.

Pete   Cos you teefed mine!

Ste *kicks* **Pete**. **Pete** *kicks* **Ste** *back.*

Ste   Baz, ask Alan if he can get us some more glue. He must have contacts.

Pete *laughs.*

Baz   Wassat mean?

Ste   Little baby Alan *must* know where to get stickies. How else did he put his cot together?

Baz   Ya wanna shut your hole, Ste.

Ste   Suck me. Ooh I forgot, ya can't, ya mouth's too dry from licking ya brother's arse!

The two square up.

Ste   What ya gonna do, faggot? Kiss me?

Baz *headbutts* **Ste**.

Pete *pushes* **Baz**.

Pete   The fuck was that for!

Baz   Who are you? His girlfriend?

Ste   You've fucking *changed*, I swear!

Baz   Just don't take the piss.

Ste   Look who's taking the piss! All you ever talk about since ya come out is ya fucking brother. Alan this. Alan that. Get real, yeah? He'll be a DJ when I'll be PM. Ya know what PM means? It means Prime fucking Minister!

Pete   Nice one.

Slight pause.

Baz   Just cos your brother died.

Pause.

Ste *lunges at* **Baz**. **Pete** *prevents* **Ste** *from getting to* **Baz**.

Baz   What's the big deal? You wanted me to get *real*!

A car goes by. **Pete** *still tries to defuse the tussle. The car stops a few metres down the road.* **Baz** *notices it. The car beeps its horn once.*

Baz   See you girls at MFI.

Baz *exits.*

Ste *pushes* **Pete** *to the floor.*

Ste   Alright!

He shouts towards the car.

Make sure he wears a rubber! He's got AIDS!

The car drives off.

Who's got the sweets?

Baz *must have them.*

Ste   Nice one, Pete.

*A man walks on (**Brian**) with a rucksack, smoking a roll-up. He wears a fleece and jeans. He has a pony-tail and a swastika tattoo on his neck, and an Iron Cross and 'hate' tattooed on his hands. He looks at the kids. They stare back. **Ste** gets to his feet.*

The kids walk round him and exit.

*He stands there and watches them leave. He stares out ahead at the road and the direction in which **Baz** left.*

He exits that way.

Snap fade.

Scene Six

Morris *and his mate* **Keith** *sit on the couch with cans of Tennent's, watching the late-night boxing.*

Val *enters from the bedroom, topless. She reaches over them to grab her fags, then sits in the armchair.*

Morris   Mum! Put them away!

Val   Mind your own business.

Morris   It's disgusting! I'm drinking!

Val   I'm feeding Alan!

Morris   Then shut the door behind ya!

Val   I'm having a cigarette break!

Beat.

I'm in between tits if you must know. I'm letting 'em breathe.

Slight pause.

Ain't you gonna introduce us?

Slight pause.

Morris   Keith Mum, Mum Keith.

Val *reaches over* **Morris** *to shake hands with the delighted* **Keith**.

Morris   Fuck sake!

Val   I've told you about swearing in the house, Morris.

Morris   No you fucking haven't! Ya doing this on purpose! Now fuck off!

Val   Don't you tell me to fuck off in my own house!

Morris *turns up the volume a bit.*

Morris   I'm sorry, mate.

Keith   No, it's fine, honest . . .

Pause.

Val   So what do you do, Keith?

Keith *(trying hard not look at her)*   Student.

Val   What ya study?

Beat.

Keith   Biology.

Morris *hits him on the arm.*

Pause.

Val   Who's fighting?

Morris   No one you know, put a top on.

Val   Who's gonna win? White or black?

Slight pause.

Keith   Black.

Slight pause.

Val   Does my left tit look sore?

Keith *masks his mouth with his hand and tries his hardest not to crack up.*

Pause.

Val   Keith, does my left tit look sore to you?

Morris *stands up and turns off the TV. He stares at* **Val**. *She stares back.*

Silence.

The baby starts to cry from the bedroom.

Val   He's hungry.

She stands up.

I'll give him the right one, shall I?

She goes into the bedroom.

Keith   I'm just gonna have a quick slash, mate. Help yourself to some more.

Keith *hurriedly walks to the toilet.*

Morris *just stands there.*

Slow fade.

Scene Seven

Ken's *flat.*

Baz *and* **Ken** *are just waking up in bed. Eyes are hard to open. Big hangovers.*

Ken *reaches over to drink from a glass of water. He offers it to* **Baz**. **Baz** *takes a sip and gives it back to* **Ken**. **Ken** *puts the glass back. They both pick the sleep out of their eyes.*

Baz *yawns and stretches, pushing* **Ken** *as he does so.* **Ken** *knocks* **Baz**'s *arm away.* **Baz** *laughs a bit. He stops suddenly, as if remembering something. He quickly checks himself under the covers. He breathes a sigh of relief and puts the cover back down.*

Ken   What?

Baz   Nothing.

Ken   Ya ain't pissed yaself?

Baz   No I ain't pissed myself. Had that dream again.

Ken   What dream?

Baz   *That* dream.

Ken *thinks for a bit.*

Baz   Waking up / as a girl?

Ken   Waking up as a girl.

Ken *laughs.*

Baz   It ain't funny! It's a nightmare!

Ken   No, course not, sorry. So . . . is it still there?

Baz   Just about.

Beat.

Ken   D'ya still cry in ya sleep?

Baz   Not no more. It's just nightmares now. Wake up, my heart's pumping like fuck.

Ken   Ya should keep away from the glue. Stick to fags.

Baz   Can't buy fags, can I? Gotta be sixteen.

Ken   Christ, when I was a kid I had to buy fags for the old man every week. I was allowed to buy these candy-cigarettes with the change. I remember the shopkeeper would say, 'A packet for your dad, and a packet for you.' All my friends had them, we'd pretend to smoke and then eat them. They started on us *young* in my day . . .

Baz   Don't do a 'my day' on me now. I just got up.

Ken   Wait, you'll like this one. There was no speed limit in my day. How about that?

Baz   Shu'up.

Ken   True.

Baz   No speed limit? Ya mean ya could drive as fast as you want?

Ken   Yep. Ya see, in my day, we were treated like adults.
No speed limit. No yellow lines. No seat-belts. No parking
meter . . .

Baz   No seat-belts?

Ken   No nothing. I remember doing over a hundred once
and this copper on a bike pulled me over and said, 'Do you
realise how fast you were going?' and I said, 'Very, I'm trying
to get back for Benny Hill,' and he said I should watch out
for my speed in future and did you see the one where he
was a gym teacher in a girls' holiday camp. I didn't have
a driver's licence on me at the time. It wasn't even my car,
it was my brother's.

Ken *gives a quick kiss on the side of* **Baz**'s *head and ruffles his hair.
He gets out of bed to go to the bathroom. He is naked. He continues
his story offstage from his bathroom. While he is out,* **Baz** *reaches over
to check* **Ken**'s *wallet on the bedside table. There is nothing in it.
Disappointed, he checks* **Ken**'s *trousers for change. He takes a few
pound coins and leaves the shrapnel. He puts the coins in his own jeans
pockets.*

Ken (*offstage*)   I remember you could smoke on the
underground. Can you imagine that happening nowadays?
There were two carriages at the front you could smoke in.
I didn't even smoke when I was a kid but there were always
tons of free seats during rush hour. Ya could smoke in
cinemas. People didn't think twice about lighting up. You
did that today you'd get ya head shot off. There were
adverts showing how cool it was to smoke, not how life-
threatening it is. I actually thought they were healthy. Sexy
and good for you. Picking up girls was easy. Literally click
your fingers. If you bought them a drink that was more or
less a signed contract for sex. Tommy Cooper snuffed it live
on stage. JFK got his brains blown out live on tele. The
Yanks put a man on the moon in a film studio and every
one believed it. It was a non-stop bloody carnival. No such
thing as terrorism. No such thing as baggage control at
airports. STDs no one got, no one knew about. AIDS didn't

exist. And after the pill, well that was it, women were *twice* more likely to get their draws off. One-night stands. Quickies round the back. They were less inhibited. No *fear* about sex. No paranoia. It was liberated. On tap if you knew where it hang out. Drinking and driving was perfectly acceptable. Open drug experimentation for the middle classes, flower power for all and sundry. Orgies. Beatles. Kinks. Stones. Those were the days, Baz. Those were the days.

Baz   Don't rub it in.

Ken *comes to the bathroom door. He wears Kermit the Frog boxer shorts.*

Baz   Oi, you know that nightmare where I turn into a girl?

Baz *takes the sheet off him and he has put his penis in between his legs so it looks as if he has a vagina. He laughs. So does* **Ken**.

Snap fade.

Scene Eight

Val*'s flat.*
Madonna *waits, biting her nails. A ring at the door. The dogs bark.*

She turns off the recording and lets in the **Policeman**.

He walks in in full uniform, takes off his helmet.

Policeman   We alone?

Madonna   What do you think I am?

Policeman   No comment.

She locks the door behind him.

You've got a shiner under your eye.

Madonna   No I ain't.

Policeman *jabs her in the face hard.*

Policeman I think you'll find you have.

Beat.

Been walking around with a semi-on all day . . . stop pretending it hurts!

Madonna Let's just do this, yeah?!

Policeman (*wagging his finger*) Uh-huh.

He draws the blinds, turns on the side-lamp and turns off the main light. He walks into the centre of the room.

Madonna, I get the faint impression you've been avoiding me. First you go AWOL, then you do the silent treatment (which is a fucking turn-on, I must say) and now I'm getting strange whiffs and whispers from the kiddies. Like I'm supposed to be expecting something. Except I don't know what it is.

Madonna Ain't got a clue. Look, I'm 'ere aren't I?

Policeman Just don't want things to get sour between us, that's all.

Pause.

Hey, I'm sorry, just me being paranoid. Come here.

She does.

Take your jacket off.

She does. Underneath, she wears a low-cut top, tight mini-skirt and high heels.

Looking good for a whore. For a nigger.

Beat.

Say it. Ni-gg-er.

Beat.

Madonna Nigger.

Policeman Ni-gg-er.

Madonna   Ni-gg-er.

Policeman   Louder.

Beat.

Madonna   Ni-gg-er!

Policeman   Like you mean it!

Madonna   Nigger!

Slight pause.

Policeman   There. That wasn't too hard, was it? Now what am I? I'm a white cunt. Say it.

Madonna   You're a dirty piece of white *shit* cunt is what you are.

Policeman   Again.

Madonna   Useless white cunt-sucker.

Policeman   I just fucked a Muslim with a Coke bottle, you can do better than that. Again!

Madonna   I don't wanna play!

Policeman   This ain't a game! Say it!

Madonna   I don't wanna!

Policeman   Say it!

Madonna   White! Cunt!

Pause.

Policeman   How d'ya feel?

Slight pause.

Madonna   Filthy.

Beat.

Policeman   Perfect. When I come I want you to keep your eyes open.

He takes off his handcuffs and drops them to the floor.

He takes out his truncheon and drops it to the floor.

He takes out a tube of lubricant and drops it to the floor.

He takes off his helmet, looks deep into it, sniffs it and drops it to the floor.

He takes out a roll of gaffer tape and drops it to the floor.

He takes out a digital camera and places it gently on the floor.

Next, he takes out a pair of cellophane gloves and puts them on.

From his back pocket he pulls out a pair of swimming goggles and puts them on.

He holds his arms open.

Policeman   Shall we?

Lights out.

Scene Nine

Baz *and* **Ken** *are sitting in a pub.* **Ken** *wears an Arsenal home top (circa 1980s) and has a pint of Guinness.* **Baz** *has a glass of Coke.*

Ken   Don't look now. Two tables behind me to the left . . . I said *don't* look now. Have you seen him before?

Baz   No.

Ken   He was in Smith's in the Broadwalk.

Baz   So?

Ken   And now he's in 'ere.

Baz   Free country.

Ken   That's where ya wrong. You know as well as I do. It ain't a free country.

Baz   Gi's a light.

Ken *lights him up.*

Ken   So. How's Alan?

Baz   Good, cheers.

Ken   Was he worth coming back for?

Baz *produces a folded-up piece of paper from his jacket and gives it to* **Ken**. *It is a drawing of* **Alan**. **Ken** *puts on his specs.*

Ken   Oh Baz. Is this him? That's . . . that's better than a photo that. This . . . you could frame that. Iron out the folds. Quality paper.

Baz   From school.

Ken   What is it? Charcoal?

Baz   Yeah.

Ken   How d'ya get the . . . ?

Baz   Smudge it with ya finger, blend it in. Easy really.

Ken   Why don't ya use colour?

Baz   It's not a painting. It's a sketch.

Ken   Hardly a sketch. It's a work of art.

Baz   A sketch-drawing. Ya can't colour-in a charcoal drawing.

Ken   Nah, course not. Be nice though.

Baz   Ain't got paints, have I? Less I do a proper job on the art room.

Ken   There must be work for this somewhere. Get a scholarship. Go to college with that.

Baz   And draw with a bunch o' tossers?

Beat.

Ken   Yeah. Gotta sign it, though. Years to come people'll look at that. Wanna know who did it. Gotta pencil?

Baz *takes a magic marker out from his pocket.*

Ken   Felt will do. Put ya signature there. Make it famous.

Baz   What, like when Val signs for school trips?

Ken   Exactly.

Baz   She never signs for school trips.

Ken   Her giro then.

Baz   Right.

Beat.

Ken   But not *her* signature. Yours.

Baz   Ain't got one.

Ken   Make one. But make sure you always stick to it.
Ya can't go changing your signature willy-nilly. It's security.
Once you've done it, that's it.

Baz   Can't I use my tag?

Ken   What is ya tag?

Baz   GranZey.

Beat.

Ken   Spell it.

Baz   G. R. A. N. Capital Z. E. Y with a little arrow thing
down the bottom.

Beat.

Ken   What the fuck is that?

Baz   Nothing. It's my tag.

Beat.

Ken   This is . . . right. (*Takes off his glasses and rubs his eyes.*)
Ya can't use ya tag, no. Ya can't tag that. It's a work of art.
Ya can't tag ya giro. Ya signature has to be ya name. Barry
Fitch. But ya can style it anyway ya want. Look, practise on
this.

Ken *takes out an old betting slip.*

Baz   I've seen signatures. They're just squiggles.

Ken   Exactly. Welcome to the real world.

Baz   Ya can't even make sense of 'em.

Ken   Ya don't have ta.

Baz   Then why does it have to be ya name?

Ken   Because . . . listen, look, listen, right. Lemme start from the beginning. (*Puts his glasses away.*) It has to be ya name or at least something that you alone can make sense of or . . . preferably . . . you alone can write. Ya don't want it to be easy or people will forge it.

Baz   Forge it?

Ken   Fake it. Copy it.

Slight pause.

Ya can't put down Crampsey!

Baz   Gran*Z*ey. With a Z. It's my tag.

Ken   No! Look, this is mine.

He writes it on the slip.

Baz   That's just a squiggle.

Ken   No it's not. Ken. K there. Jameson.

Baz   That is not a K.

Ken   What it is then?

Baz   A small B.

Beat.

Be Jennifer. Says there. Ya right. There's no way anyone's gonna copy *that*. 'S awful.

Ken   Just . . . (*Pushes the drawing to* **Baz**.) Take that with ya and think about it.

Baz   That's yours. I drew it for you.

Ken   Really? Thank you.

Slight pause.

Baz   D'ya want my autograph?

Ken   Don't start.

He looks at the drawing again.

Your mum let ya pick him up yet?

Baz   Nah, not really. She lets me do the shit stuff like change the nappy, hold the bottle upright. I pick him up behind her back. She's got this wild fantasy that I'm gonna drop him on his head. Must be feeling guilty 'bout something. No wonder Morris is a bit slow. She'll come round soon. Won't have a choice, will she?

Ken   Ya really like the nipper.

Baz   Always wanted a little brother.

Ken   So what is he now? A DJ or a footballer, I forget.

Baz   He was never a footballer. Gonna get him 'My First Decks' from Tomy. For his birthday.

Ken   When is it?

Baz   September the tenth.

Ken   What sign is that?

Baz   It's the sign of September. September the tenth.

Ken   You see, I think it's you who really wants to be the DJ.

Baz   Nah. Too old for that now. Wouldn't know the first thing.

Ken   What *do* you wanna be then? After school.

Baz   Left alone.

Ken   Seriously.

Slight pause.

Baz   Nothing.

Ken *lights up a fag.*

Ken   How *is* school?

Baz   What is this? Twenty questions?

Ken   Oi, don't get lippy. You've jacked it in, intcha.

Baz   No shit, Sherlock.

Ken   They'll put you back in the home.

Baz   Not now. I'm what they call 'indispensable'. Val needs me to look after Al. If it weren't for me . . .

Ken   If it weren't for you she'd get some other mug. It's between a rock and hard place and you gotta choose. Which is it?

Baz   You ain't my dad.

Ken   Baz . . .

Ken *reaches for* **Baz**'s *hand but* **Baz** *pulls away.*

Beat.

You ain't wearing the present I gave ya.

Baz   What present?

Ken   You mean ya sold it already? The Christmas present.

Silence.

Is he still looking at me?

Baz   Why? Ya fancy him?

Ken   Don't be daft. He's too old.

Baz   Can we go now?

Ken   You can go whenever ya like. Free country.

Baz *gives him a look. That's not what he wanted to hear.* **Baz** *leaves.*

Ken   Baz . . . wait . . .

He looks behind him. He looks on after **Baz**. *He drains his pint and slams the glass on the table.*

Lights out.

Scene Ten

The flat.

Baz *lets himself in. There is no one at home. It is Christmas Day. He opens the cupboards. They are all bare except for a tin of baked beans and some left-over bread. He takes the last piece of bread and toasts it. He tries to work the hob, but the gas is down and he hasn't got any tokens to put in the meter.*

He finds a nearly-empty box of Christmas crackers in a cupboard and takes one out.

He opens the tin and when the toast pops up he pours the cold beans on the toast and takes the plate over to the couch. He turns on the TV. On comes the TV announcer spouting Merry Christmas messages and introducing Bedknobs and Broomsticks.

He pulls the cracker himself and puts on the hat. There is no spark. He takes out the spark paper itself and snaps it. Again, no bang. He reads the joke without any reaction and puts the pointless little plastic toy on his lap. He puts a blanket that is on the couch around his shoulders for some warmth. He slowly eats the meal and stares blankly at the TV with a general air of indifference.

Suddenly, the meter runs out, the box makes a rattling sound and the lights and TV go out.

Darkness.

Scene Eleven

The flat. The dogs are in mid-bark. **Madonna** *answers the door and lets in the* **Policeman**. *He is in civvies.* **Madonna** *remains standing, her face is still slightly bruised from Scene Eight.*

Policeman (*holding her face to the light*)   For Chrissake. Who did this? Madonna. Listen, you can't carry on like this. You won't be grassing. Just tell me who did this and I'll sort them out.

He turns away and walks to the couch, smirking to himself.

Where's the champagne? I got it.

Slight pause.

I'm on duty.

Slight pause.

As we speak.

Slight pause.

Plain-clothes copper.

Slight pause.

You know what that means, don't you?

Silence.

I want a cuddle.

Madonna *slowly and purposefully gives him the finger.*

Policeman   Come along. That's no way to treat a trick.

Madonna   You ain't a trick no more. Ya never was.

Policeman   I really don't want to start being energetic. I've had a hard day cleaning up after you lot. Now stop acting like a coon and give me a cuddle.

He holds his arms open.

Gerbil *walks out from the bedroom. He carries a blind man's walking stick in front of him. He is the tallest and fattest man you ever saw. Quite possibly a giant. He wears a black mink coat, medallions, gold rings and sunglasses. He just about fits through the door. He stands there.* **Policeman** *is evidently unnerved. There is a long silence.*

Policeman   Alright, Gerbil?

Silence.

So this is what it's been about. Got to hand it to you, I'd never have guessed. Never had thought you'd . . . Madge, I've known you for years, come on.

Silence. **Madonna** *looks away, she is saddened it has come to this.*

Policeman   I get the message.

He walks to the door.

Guess I'll see you on the other side.

Madonna   Not if I've got anything to do with it.

Slight pause.

Policeman   That's the spirit.

He leaves.

More silence.

Madonna   Thanks, Gerb. I'm sorry I had to waste ya time but you're the only guy, ya know? I never wanted it to come to this but . . . ya know the rest. Jerry said that this deserved you, you spoke to him, didn't you? . . . Course ya did . . .

As soon as **Madonna** *starts speaking* **Gerbil** *contracts his walking stick and puts it in his pocket. He starts to undo his belt and his jeans buttons.*

Madonna *dutifully starts to undo her jeans.*

Slow fade.

Scene Twelve

Late at night. **Val** *is asleep on the couch with a half-empty bottle of whisky in her hand. An empty bottle of vodka sits on the table in front of her.*

Baz *enters. He checks the dog-barking box. Its wires have been pulled out. He smiles appreciatively. He notices* **Val**. *He goes over and gently takes the bottle from her hand. He puts the empty bottle in the bin and, after thinking about it, drains the remainder of the whisky bottle in the sink and bins that too.*

He goes back to **Val**, *takes the blanket on the couch and puts it on her. He closes her mouth and gives her a soft kiss on the forehead. She reacts to this in her sleep, smiles and murmurs something loving.* **Baz** *tucks her hair behind her ear and looks at her.*

He goes up to the cot. **Alan** *isn't there. He notices sounds coming from his bedroom. He opens the door. Lights slowly up on* **Madonna** *breast-feeding* **Alan**. **Baz** *looks on. He has known the true situation for some time. He feels relieved.* **Madonna** *has her back to him. She doesn't hear or notice him.*

Scene Thirteen

Ken *sits in a woolly hat and scarf feeding the ducks by the pond.*

Baz *enters in the background and looks on.* **Ken** *can't see him.*

Silence.

Ken   Ever get the feeling ya being watched?

Baz   Only during lunch break.

He sits down on the far end of the bench.

Didn't know if we were talking or not.

Pause.

Where've ya been? Ya don't come to the stretch no more.

Ken   It's the missus. Christmas and that.

Baz   Lies.

Pause.

Freezing. Only one in the park, you are.

Ken   S'way I like it.

Baz   Who ya throwing that to? Ain't no ducks.

Ken   They'll come.

Slight pause.

There's this fox come round the back sometimes.

Baz   Gonna hog that all day, then?

Ken *reluctantly chucks the loaf of bread over to* **Baz***.*

Baz *starts to eat the bread.*

Ken *snatches it back.*

Ken   Oi! Whatcha doing?!

Baz   I'm 'ungry!

Ken   It's for the ducks! Only got a bit left. How would you like it if they ate *your* bread?

Baz   They *are* eating my bread. That doesn't even make any sense anyway. What ya chatting 'bout? Imaginary ducks eating bread I haven't even got? What planet you on?

Ken   You can have a piece. There.

Baz *takes the piece and shows* **Ken** *that he is throwing it to the ducks. He nibbles pieces now and then.*

Baz   Saw ya Christmas Day eating with the family. Curtains were closed but there was a gap I could see in. Don't worry, no one could see me. I wasn't gonna ring the bell or nuffink. But it was weird, I just stood outside. Ya wife ain't *that* old. Thought she looked nice. Was this close to ya. Funny watching you like that. Weird, ya know?

Ken   Dincha go to ya nan's?

Baz   Left soon as I got there. Was doing my head in. Nan's new fella. Not a nice man.

Ken   What did Val say?

Baz   Didn't care. Too busy with Alan.

Ken   That's good, innit? 'S what ya came back for. From the home. Make sure Alan was being looked after properly.

Baz   It's not Val I'm worried about. It's Madge.

Ken   How come?

Beat.

Baz   Long story.

Slight pause.

Hey, I didn't just come back to check up on Al, ya know. I missed ya, didn't I?

Silence.

Baz *reaches over to tap him on the head.*

Hello? Anyone home . . . ?

Ken *reels away.*

Baz   What's wrong?

Ken   People around.

Baz   So? No one knows who we are.

Beat.

You could be my dad for all they care.

Ken *looks at him, stony-faced.* **Baz** *looks away.*

Baz   So what ya doing New Year's? I was thinking . . .

Ken   Look. What did I tell ya? The ducks are coming.

Baz *gently throws his bread to the ground and looks down. The entire length of the bench between them.*

Pause.

Snap fade.

Scene Fourteen

Muzzy *and* **Karim** *are in the flat smoking crack out of an adapted can of Coke.* **Val** *is lying on the floor coming out of a big downer. We can hear the sounds of the couple fighting next door.*

Muzzy   And then they tie her up and he takes out a cucumber and puts a condom on it.

Karim   You what?

Muzzy   Exactly. Then he bones her with it.

Karim   Don't, man.

Muzzy   *Gang Bang Granny*, it's a classic.

Karim   Where do I get it?

Muzzy   Tel sells 'em on Sunday market. Go up and say 'home video', he knows what you mean.

Silence. They smoke.

Karim   They ever gonna hush up?

Muzzy   Who?

Karim   Next door.

Muzzy   Oh. Yes? I don't know.

Beat.

Look at her.

Muzzy *mounts* **Val** *and simulates sex.*

Karim *simulates recording them on a video camera.*

Karim   Give me romantic.

Muzzy *does so.*

Karim   Give me sexy.

Muzzy *does so.*

Karim   Give me doggy.

Muzzy *does so.*

Val *pushes him away.*

Karim   Leave it, man, she well out.

Muzzy *puts finger to lips and says 'Sssh' as he excitedly goes up to the cot.*

Muzzy   Let's have an ickle look at Junior.

He opens the cot top up.

Aaaah. Got my nose.

Karim   Nose for what? Charlie?

Muzzy   Shu'up. Got her chin. Got my mouth.

Karim   All the better to cuss you with.

Karim *laughs.*

Muzzy   Got a fat stomach. Must be a greedy guts.

Karim   Get that from you.

Muzzy   Get that from *you.*

Karim   Don't be saying shit like that.

Muzzy *puts his hands in the cot.*

Muzzy   Ras. He ain't got my cock.

Karim   Give it a few years.

Muzzy   No, I mean ain't got my cock. He's all hooded up.

Karim *takes another hit from the crack can and gets up to see.*

Karim   Le's see. Aah man, dat's rank.

Muzzy   My Junior ain't gonna grow up wid an ugly cock.

Karim   Who says he's *your* Junior?

Muzzy   You gotta be doing these things when they still young. So they can't feel it when they older. Hey, Val, get up. Bad enough you gotta give a boy a white man's name now you giving him a white man's cock.

She can't hear him.

Get her up 'ere.

Karim   She's gone, I told you.

Muzzy   Breaks my heart, man.

Karim   He ain't a Muslim, Muzzy. Look at him.

Muzzy   What does a Muslim look like?

Karim   I dunno.

Muzzy   Precise. You tell a Muslim by his cock.

Beat.

Karim   And a Jew.

Muzzy   HE AIN'T A FUCKING JEW.

Val *stirs and mumbles.*

Muzzy   Nothing, Val, you go back to bed. Me and Karim having a . . . spiritual conversation.

Karim   You ain't religious.

Muzzy   Got zip to do wid religion. It's *tradition*. It's a father-son thing. Passed down from generation to generation.

Karim   Don't be giving me dat. It's cos you know women prefer a roundhead. No smegma. No smell. Hygienic. Girls floss their teeth wid it all day.

Muzzy   Dat too. I'm not having no son o' mine doing 50p coin tricks wid his foreskin.

Karim Yeah? Get used to it. This ickle whitey's gonna be pissing all over ya fat dick at The Hart with his foreskin spray. Pssssh. Pssssh. He'll be playing peek-a-boo wid his white Christian girlfriends.

Muzzy Get me da blade.

Karim *stops laughing.*

Karim It's too big for dat. What you riffing 'bout?

Muzzy Kaz, da blade.

Slight pause.

Karim Have another hit. Chill. It's New Year.

Muzzy *goes into his jacket pocket and pulls out a large, rusty old flick-knife. He goes back to the cot.*

Karim (*giggling*) Oh Val?

Muzzy Hush up. She got nuffink do wid dis.

Karim You serious?

Muzzy You wanna know what a Muslim look like?

Karim I don't want it to start crying again, man.

Muzzy Be crying for right reasons. Be crying for Allah.

Karim Like you know whatta do.

Muzzy I seen 'em do it before.

Karim Like where?

Muzzy Like all my cousins when I was a kid.

Karim (*smiling*) This is dark.

Muzzy Distract it.

Karim Who?

Muzzy Da baby!

Karim How am I gonna distract it?! I think it's gonna know what's happening!

Muzzy *flicks the knife open.*

Karim   Oh man!

Karim *squirms on the spot, looking at* **Val** *and back at* **Muzzy**.

Snap fade.

Scene Fifteen

The following morning. **Baz** *comes home to the flat. He checks the cot.* **Alan** *is in it. The flat smells very bad.*

Baz   Val!

Pause.

Val! The baby's shit himself!

Beat.

You hum, you know that? How long have you been humming there for? Eh?

He goes into the bedrooms.

Mum?

He comes out. The flat is empty. He walks out of the front door. He comes back in after a while. He's angry that the baby has been left on his own. He checks on the fridge for any notes left. Nothing. He has to change the baby's nappy himself. He picks up a fresh nappy.

Baz   Right, you little shitter. I'm gonna breathe through my mouth, I suggest you do the same.

As soon as **Baz** *takes off the dirty nappy his face drops. He stares closer. Horror creeps over his face. He turns round to vomit into the sink. He splashes water onto his face and hair and swills his mouth out. He begins to sob. He steadies himself on the kitchen counter.*

Slow fade.

Scene Sixteen

The bridge by the canal. **Ken** *is sharing a joint with* **Ste**. **Baz** *rushes on in tears.*

Baz   Ken! Fuck off, Ste, I wanna talk to Ken.

Ste   You fuck off, I was 'ere first.

Baz   Ste, don't start now, please.

Ste   Why ya crying? They gonna put ya back in the castle?

Baz *lunges for* **Ste** *but* **Ken** *breaks them up.*

Ken   Oi! Both of ya can fuck off if ya gonna be like that!

Baz   Ken, I'm serious. I need to talk.

Ste   Need something else more like. Do you know what he said to me last time?

Ken   Ste, I think you better go. I'll see ya later, yeah? Keep the joint.

Ste *realises* **Baz** *is serious.*

Ste   What is it ya can tell him that ya can't tell me?

Baz   Just . . . stuff.

Ste   Thought we were mates.

Baz   We are.

Ste   Mates don't do this.

Ste *pulls back his hair to reveal a slight cut on his forehead.*

Ken (*to* **Baz**)   That was you?

Beat.

Ste   For your information. My brother never died. He just hasn't come back yet, that's all. (*To* **Ken**.) Look after him yeah. Fuck knows he needs *some*one.

Ste *exits.*

Ken *looks at* **Baz**.

Baz   They did it. They fucking cut him. It's all mash down there.

Ken   Whoah there, slow down, did what? Who did what?

Baz   I don't know who. Whoever comes in the flat. Went to change the nappy and . . . down there . . . all red . . . just a pulp . . . He looked fine though . . . He was smiling . . . he was smiling at me the poor cunt . . . What d'he do to deserve that? . . . eh?

Ken   Come 'ere.

Baz   No . . . No, fuck off . . . I shoulda been there . . . I shoulda stopped it . . . It's a joke . . . a fucking circus . . . the lot of 'em . . . and now Alan . . . Why him? . . . What he ever do? Live?! . . .

Ken   It's not your fault.

Baz   It's probably Madonna . . . She couldn't fucking stand the sight of him . . . her own son . . .

Ken   Baz . . .

Baz   You know as well as I do . . . any other girl her age would be chuffed to have a kid like that . . . it's cos she got *raped*, that's why she did it . . . Makes sense dunit, take it out on *him* . . .

Ken   Baz you don't have to tell me this . . .

Baz   Nah, you're wrong Ken, I *do* have ta. I'm telling ya and you're gonna listen and you're gonna shut the fuck up! Balls only dropped last year and I'm an uncle . . . a fucking uncle . . . I heard it long before the rest of the estate . . . so don't even start . . . She got cornered by two boys and a girl at school . . . at *school* . . . during lunch break . . . I even know the boys, they're brothers, MacLeishes, two years below me, my age but they got held back, one of 'em lives on Quakers . . . They ain't even been caught . . . not even Morris went after 'em . . . he doesn't care no more . . .

Morris . . . (*Beat.*) Morris and Mum. I never told no one.
I'm telling *you*. A few years ago. Was probably twelve. She'd
picked him up from The Hart, he went to lock-ins there,
had a ruck once, they came back and started fighting again,
trying to be quiet but I could hear 'em, so could Madge. My
door wouldn't shut properly cos the handle was bust so I
could see into the living room . . . I could see the couch . . .
They . . . they . . . (*Beat.*) I saw the whole thing, Ken . . . it
went on for ages . . . Wanted to get up . . . start crying or
something . . . but I couldn't . . . couldn't speak . . . couldn't
move . . . Just put my face into the pillow and turned away
. . . Madge had her duvet over her head . . . That's why
they never talk to each other, Mum and Morris . . . ever
since then they've never really . . . and I've had enough . . .
fucking had enough . . .

Ken   Baz. Ya can't be sure. You were young . . .

Baz   Young?! When was I ever *young*?! Eh? Tell me. When
have I ever been a kid, a child? Never. I'd stay in school if I
didn't get hassled so much . . . I *would*, you know I would . . .
Listen, lemme tell ya, I was gonna walk . . . tonight . . . this
night . . . I was gonna leave Val some cash . . . some cash
for Alan . . . was gonna talk to Madge . . . get it out in the
open . . . I reckon she'll come round eventually, ya know? . . .
Had enough money for a ticket to Brighton . . . one way . . .
Few of the lads said they knew a place I could stay . . .
The only reason I went back there tonight was to get my
birth certificate so I could get a passport and get the fuck
out of this country . . . Val didn't even know I *had* a birth
certificate . . . probably used it for filters when she ran
out . . .

Silence.

That's it . . . that's all I wanted to say . . . Oh, and you can
come with me if you like.

Slight pause.

Ken   Come with you where?

Baz I can't leave him there. With them. He's my
responsibility now. We can get away. You, me and Alan.
All three of us. No one would know. They wouldn't care
anyway. I'll leave them a letter with the cash in it. I'll tell
them it's for the best. I've spent all my life running away
from one place to the next. I don't want Alan to do the same.
This is it. This'll be the fresh start. The new beginning. You
always said you wanted a little boy. You can be the dad . . .
I'll be the mum . . .

Ken Baz . . .

Baz We could start a family. A proper one . . .

Ken Barry.

Baz Get a place out in the country . . . We do it properly
they'll never find us . . .

Ken Barry, please . . .

Baz At least give it a go, ya know what I mean?

Ken Barry.

Baz The SS don't give a shit no more . . . trust me, we
could *do* this . . . I've been thinking 'bout it for ages . . . but
this is it . . . now's the time . . . Please . . . please don't say
no . . . I love you . . . please . . . (*He begins to cry.*) Tell me
you'll help me . . . please, Ken . . . that you'll help me . . .
I'm scared Ken . . . I'm scared . . . fuck, I'm scared . . .

Baz goes to **Ken**. **Ken** *holds him as he cries.*

Ken Come 'ere.

They hold each other for a while. **Ken** *rocks* **Baz** *gently.*

Ken Don't cry . . . you'll make *me* cry . . . How come you
get to be the mummy . . . eh? . . . This plan of yours . . .
looks like you were doing a lot of thinking when ya were
away . . . And where do ya plan to go once you've got this
passport? . . . Day trip to France? . . . Bangkok? . . . The
Ivory Coast?

Baz (*muffled*)   Australia.

Ken   Oh, *Australia* . . . shoulda guessed . . . is that far enough for you, ya think?

Baz *laughs reluctantly and playfully hits him a bit.*

Ken   Look, Baz, look at me.

Ken *turns* **Baz***'s face to look at him.*

Ken   What is my advice worth to you?

Baz   Everything.

Ken   Cos I've known you a long time and I get a funny feeling whatever I say ya gonna go right ahead and do what you wanna do.

Beat.

Am I right?

Baz *nods.*

Ken   Right. So I'm gonna help ya.

Baz *goes to cuddle* **Ken***.* **Ken** *holds* **Baz** *off.*

Ken   Hey, hold on! Hear me out first. Who's at home with Alan now?

Baz   No one probably.

Ken   Well, first things first. Go home. Write a letter to Val . . .

Baz   She can't read.

Ken   Can Madonna?

Baz   Yeah.

Ken   Write it to Val, Madonna can read it to her. Say what's happened to Alan and that you're taking him to hospital.

Baz   They'll take him away from her, from *me* . . . !

Ken   We don't know that. You leave that to me. I'll spin
a story . . .

Baz   Cos if that happened then I might as well . . . !

Ken   No one's taking no one away, OK? Look at me, I said
look at me. Right. Deep breaths. Come on. OK? Now don't
leave too much cash cos she'll only smoke it. Wrap up the
kid in whatever it is Val usually takes him out in. Bring his
bottle, a few toys, whatever keeps him happy. And come and
meet me here. I'll have the car running. Now listen, hey, if
no one's home then it's important you bring him to me as
soon as you can. I need to see what's happened with my
own eyes. Alright? If there's so much as a scratch we're
taking him to hospital, do I make myself clear . . . ?

Baz   We can patch him up ourselves . . .

Ken   Are you a doctor? Didn't think so. Don't worry, I'll
say I'm his dad. We'll only stay there as long as we need to.

Baz   Then we go away, right? Straight off.

Ken   Once the kid's sorted, we're all going on a summer
holiday.

Baz   I'm serious, Ken.

Beat.

Ken   So am I. We'll go somewhere. Alan too. Fresh start.

Baz   Ya mean it?

Ken   Not abroad, no, I'm not stupid. Nothing drastic.
Just . . . somewhere. Some time out.

Baz *smiles.*

Baz   Come with me.

Ken   I daren't. People might be there. And anyway, Val's
probably back already.

Baz   Not if I get there first.

Ken *gives* **Baz** *a fatherly slap.*

Ken   Good man. Off ya go. I'll get the car and come straight back. Don't let it get too dark.

Baz *smiles at* **Ken** *appreciatively and optimistically. He makes to leave.* **Ken** *puts on his jacket.* **Baz** *stops and turns back.*

Baz   Ken.

Slight pause.

Thank you.

Ken   You just go.

Baz *runs off.*

Ken *looks on with a sense of pride and protection. He waits to see* **Baz** *disappear into the distance. He thinks to himself. He looks up at the sky. Starting to get dark. He takes out his mobile phone, dials a number and waits. Checking behind him every now and then.*

Scene Seventeen

Baz *is in the flat writing a letter. The couple next door are at it again. Even more violent than before.* **Baz** *is having problems with the letter. He simply writes 'Sorry' in big letters and puts it in the envelope. He puts a few pound notes in too, and seals the letter. He writes 'Val' on the letter and props it up on the kitchen counter. He puts the last of* **Alan**'s *stuff into a kitbag and zips it up. He carefully takes* **Alan**, *all wrapped up, out of the cot, puts his hood on, picks up the bag, takes one last look at the flat and leaves.*

*The row next door is now raging. Plates are being smashed. We can clearly hear voices cussing each other in the worst terms. We hear some heavy punches. Suddenly, a thirty-year-old woman (***Katie***) crashes through the wall. She lands in* **Val**'s *living room. Plaster all over her. She is dazed.* **Steven**, *her fella, walks up to the hole in the wall; he is wearing only underpants. He can't believe what's happened.* **Katie** *gathers her senses and slowly sits up. They look at each other in quiet disbelief, then . . .* **Katie** *picks herself up and starts unhooking the toaster and kettle.* **Steven** *jumps through the partition, puts the chain on the front door and picks up the television. He puts it in his flat next*

door and comes back for the cot, checking there's nothing in it. **Katie**
chucks the kettle and toaster into the cot and goes into the bedrooms.
She comes out with a small ghetto blaster and a handful of CDs and
rushes back across the wall while **Steven** *takes a last quick look*
around the room.

Katie   Bedrooms done, come on.

Steven   Bathroom cabinet?

Katie   Shit.

She rushes back.

Steven   Quick.

Steven *opens the fridge. He takes out the contents and throws them*
through the hole in the wall: some economy cheese and a can of
Tennent's.

Katie *comes back with some pills in a bottle and some other pills in*
a carton. She jumps back into her flat.

Katie   Come on then.

Steven *notices the letter on the kitchen counter. He picks it up, thinks*
a bit, then puts it back. He starts to walk away but suddenly changes
his mind and opens the letter. His eyes light up. He pockets the money
making sure **Katie** *isn't watching him.*

Katie (*offstage*)   Come on then!

Steven *makes a slapdash effort to take the table through the hole in*
the wall but it is too big. He leaves it and jumps through the hole.

Snap fade.

Scene Eighteen

The bridge. Later that evening. **Baz** *enters carrying* **Alan** *and a*
kitbag. Sitting where **Ken** *was sitting is* **Brian** *from the Social*
Services (from end of Scene Five). He still wears the same clothes, but
no rucksack. **Baz** *stops in his tracks. They stare at each other in*

silence. **Baz** *watches* **Brian** *casually finish off his rollie and stub it out on the ground.*

Brian   Long time no see.

Baz   What you doing 'ere?

Brian   Was gonna ask you the same thing.

Pause.

Baz   Going for a walk.

Brian   Thought you'd take the baby along?

Pause.

Baz   Too noisy at the flat.

Brian   Can imagine. Don't you think it's too cold for a baby to be out tonight?

Baz   No.

Brian   What's in the bag?

Baz   What the *fuck* are you doing here?

Brian   Only . . . from where I'm standing, it looks like you're taking your baby brother on a little trip . . .

Baz   It's not that late. He needs some air.

Brian   And Val's OK with that is she?

Baz   Course. Go back and ask her yourself.

Brian   Emma's on her way there now. You remember Emma, don't you, Barry?

Baz   Don't call me that, I told ya.

Brian   Sorry. Baz.

Silence. **Baz** *puts his bag down.*

Brian   Coincidence, isn't it? Meeting you here. I often come here to get away from things my*self.*

Baz *keeps* **Alan** *tight to his chest.*

Brian   You waiting for friends or . . . ?

Baz *twigs.*

Brian You don't have to tell me if you don't want to.

Silence.

Can I have a look at the little monster?

Brian *approaches him.*

Baz Stay where you are.

Brian Come on, Baz. Just a peek.

Baz You'll wake him. Leave it.

Pause.

Brian I'll come clean. I was waiting for you. Truth is, we got a tip-off from someone claiming to be a friend of yours . . . Well, not us strictly, but the police. They've been kind enough to liaise with us on this one.

Baz Dunno what you're on about.

Brian A man in his forties, fifties? Didn't leave a name. Said you were planning on taking your brother on a little holiday. Don't blame you, wouldn't mind getting away my*self* . . .

Baz I dunno a man.

Brian Thought maybe he might be family. Family friend?

Baz *shakes his head. He can't physically speak. He knows it has to be* **Ken**.

Brian It'll probably come to you. Important thing is we got the call. I'd hate not to know where you were off to. So would Val. In fact, she's at Edgware General now. Getting her stomach pumped. She wants her baby. I think we should all go together to the hospital, don't you?

Pause.

Baz D'ya know what he's called?

Brian Who?

Baz Who d'ya think?!

Brian Right. No.

Baz Alan.

Pause.

Brian That's a / nice name . . .

Baz Always thought it was a bit of a soft name, myself.
No one's called Alan no more, are they? Not around 'ere
anyway . . .

Brian Think it's a rather nice name, had a cousin called . . .

Baz Named after Alan Smith. Not the Man U one, the
Arsenal one. Never knew him that well, just before my
time . . . Val said he had a big nose and was good with his
head . . . used to knock 'em in from the corner . . . tap-ins
from the six-yard box . . . He was her favourite . . .

Brian Can I hold him . . . ?

Baz So maybe this one'll be good with his head . . . who
knows . . . I say he's gonna be a DJ . . . not a shit pub one
on Friday nights but a proper one . . . R & B . . . drum 'n
bass . . . I prefer hip-hop with a bit o' garage . . . but it's up
to him really, innit.

Brian (*arms open*) Just for a bit . . .

Baz So . . . anyway . . . he'll get me in for free . . . up
West . . . Clapham . . . shit like that . . . and I can invite
whoever I want . . . I can have my own birthday party . . .
and even if no one comes it won't matter cos the place'll
be packed anyway . . . and anyway I'll have mates from all
over cos I'll be brothers with the most pukka DJ in town . . .
ain't that right . . .

*The more **Baz** gets worked up, the more he starts to shake the baby up
and down.*

Brian You're not holding him properly . . .

Baz I could be his manager . . . cos you see I *have* been
thinking 'bout this . . . I've even been saving up for it . . .

It'll be years from now I know . . . but . . . but that doesn't mean I can't try and save up for some decks . . . even an old crappy one and try and fix it . . .

Brian Don't shake him like that *please* . . .

Baz So if I go back now . . . home . . . or hospital . . . she won't . . . she won't . . .

Brian She *will*.

Baz She won't listen to me . . . she'll never hear my side . . . and it wasn't me who mashed him up, the poor fucker . . .

Brian Just, if you give me the baby . . .

Baz It was *her* . . . her . . . and no one'll believe me . . .

Brian Baz, listen to me, it's for his own good . . .

Baz And then you'll put me back in the home . . . and I fucking hate that . . . it's worse than the fucking flat . . . and the fosters . . . soon as someone younger comes along they kick me out . . . end up back 'ere . . . do it all over again . . .

Baz bursts into tears.

Brian What if I give you my word, Baz? If I could just check Alan's OK . . .

Baz GIVE ME BACK KEN FIRST! WHERE THE FUCK IS HE?!

Brian Ken. I don't . . . is he your friend / who phoned us . . . ?

Baz He was gonna teach me how to drive! He was gonna teach me how to drive!

Brian I understand that, really I do, but please hold him with two hands. You really must listen to me here, Baz.

A police car rolls up in the distance. Its lights keep flashing.

Baz He was gonna buy me a shaving kit! When I told him I felt queasy doing it the first time, he said he'd show me how it was done.

Brian *I'll* show you how it's done, how 'bout that?

Baz I don't *want* you to show me! I wanna speak to Ken!

Brian We'll try to find him, I swear. Baz. The baby.

Long pause. **Baz** *notices the police car.*

Baz *looks at* **Alan**.

Baz Promise you'll look after him.

Brian I promise.

Baz When he gets narky he likes to have his forehead stroked . . . between the eyes . . . up with your thumb . . .

Brian Of course . . .

Baz No . . . fucking listen to me . . . what did I just say?

Brian About when he gets narky.

Beat.

Baz Ye-es . . . ?

Brian He likes to have the forehead stroked . . . I forget / the rest of what . . .

Baz Between the eyes and up . . . with the thumb . . . It's difficult at first . . . but that's what makes him quiet down . . . he goes to sleep if you do it enough . . . If he's crying that's a different thing . . . then you're fucked.

Brian I get it . . .

Baz I haven't fucking finished yet . . . I swear if you take one step closer . . .

Brian *motions to the* **Policewoman** *in the background not to come any closer.*

Brian I'm not Baz, / I'm listening to you . . .

Baz And after you feed him with the milk bottle . . . You gotta do it properly . . . gotta be the right temperature, otherwise he won't take it . . . he's a fussy fucker . . . but he likes you to pull faces, make noises with ya mouth, clicking sounds like . . . (*Demonstrates.*) Ya can do that, can't you?

Brian   I can, yes.

Baz   Lemme see ya.

Brian *does so.*

Baz   Not that fast.

Brian *slows down.*

Baz   Better. But tell . . . ya gotta tell whoever gets him about the clicking and the forehead trick cos they won't know otherwise, I'm the only one . . .

Baz *looks at* **Alan**.

Baz   The only one . . . He's smiling, see? Look at his face. Look at his face.

Brian *goes up to* **Baz** *slowly and takes the baby from him.*

Brian   There we go. Who's a brave boy, then?

Baz *gives* **Brian** *the kitbag.*

Baz   His stuff.

Brian   Thanks.

Beat.

Baz, I'm gonna find you later and we're gonna have a proper chat, alright? I won't take no for an answer.

Brian *walks off with* **Alan**. **Baz** *walks over to where* **Ken** *would've been standing. The* **Policewoman** *looks on in the background. She gives him some time to himself. Now and again her walkie-talkie sounds.*

He looks up at the moon. Takes a deep breath. He eventually walks off to the **Policewoman**. *They exit together. The faint sounds of dogs barking. A car alarm. Perhaps a distant firecracker. Hues of red and blue flashing in the background. It's almost picturesque.*

Slow fade.